this peace

Robyn Cairns

this peace

this peace
ISBN 978 1 76041 921 9

First published 2020 by
GINNINDERRA PRESS
PO Box 3461 Port Adelaide 5015 Australia
www.ginninderrapress.com.au

For my dear Ewan
Always find a place in nature to be at peace.

In memory of my dear Dad, Rex

A feather is a piece of sky treasure.

For the poets and the dreamers

all the times
I read the sky
this peace

industrial skyline –
where the rain
makes rust

suburban roses –
a different love story
in every garden

crossed wires –
one bird seeks
the soft mottled sky

old fence
leaning away
from yesterday –
ivy sprawls
across the shade

where a house
once stood –
a patch of grass
which always
shimmers

a fruit bat
devours the warm
sweet night –
leftover pieces
of moon at my feet

layer
upon
layer

under street light
the paperbark tree

I love

summer lullaby –
the buzz of corner
street lights

rainy day –
mapping
the house spiders

wild weather
a daffodil
kisses the ground

last of the sun –
the flitting about
of honeyeaters

cricket moon
bringing the clothes in

rain on the way –
brushing against
lemon verbena

boundaries –
a caterpillar chooses
to stay inside

on a precipice –
planning to forge a new heart
for my father

strength of one cricket's song –
autumn night

reading a map
of my father's old heart –
the many treks
and trails
of love

honeyeater alights
a reed tip
these tiny poems
on a still
grey morning

heavy downpour –
the drowned out noise
of my mind

grey felted sky
turtle doves
in deep discussion

paddling the river
the peace
of every ripple

laying out
funeral clothes –
the scarf with the field
of daisies
for dad

at the supermarket –
my broken heart
a secret

climbing my mountain
of grief –
each place I rest
a new trail
appears

sympathy cards –
reminders this is real

lonely night –
playing your voice
like a pianola

little bird lingers –
I search for signs
of my dad

Hearts

I place the red camellia petal to cover my palm. The heart-shaped petal is slightly bruised. Petal on skin I contemplate hearts. Hearts break, become damaged, can be fragile, pump blood, can be cut into cookie dough, be worn on a sleeve or edible bracelet. Hearts can stop dead. The camellia petal on the damp grass begins its decay with a bruise soon to help new life grow. Dad's heart is now ash drifting across the river valley.

between the lines
the fog
of grief

stitch of spores
the time lapse of life

along the track –
just the grasses
whispering

rain-soaked moss –
kangaroo ferns
rake the fog

before dawn –
the quiet
of the world

forest moon –
a clarinet
plays softly

under swinging legs –
the pulsing light
of jellyfish

cycling the foreshore
I give my smile
to strangers

wild ocean –
the zen glide
of a pelican

pacific gull –
wind pulls me up
I soar high above
sand dunes stretching
forever

mist over water
the shape
of an egret –
stories I've known
since a child

finding solace –
dead fennel against
a dusk sky

hidden strength –
the transparent cells
of honeycomb

4 a.m. hush
our bicycle spokes
collect the last stars

floating
in a warm lake
of birdsong
the moon halved
in a sea of blue

telephone wires
slicing the moon –
the half memory
of a voiced loved
long ago

scent of fennel
in rain
and the soft
silver ribbon
of my river

sunset sky
all 1950s pastels
scrambled with grey –
southward sky
all heavy metal music

Letting Go

The place you live. The home of your heart. The heart is your home. Letting go. This year I learnt to do this a little bit better. Letting go. And for someone like me it's hard to let go. It just is. Sentimental. So, so sentimental. That feather I found five years ago on that empty beach filled with everything. The letting go makes the memories even more vivid. The scent of flowers in your childhood garden, the shade from the tree no longer there. The conversations you had with your father now clearer, your teenager's hugs that linger all day. The letting go as bird lifts to the sky to soar.

goodbyes –
I kiss the leaves
of our old tree

Mungo

Senses explode – implode, exploring the desert escarpment of a lake which overflowed with life some fifteen thousand years ago. I list the new plants I learn of. These plants are older than any time we know. They belong in the Dreaming not paper notebooks. My fingertips sweep leaves in wonder. The soft silvers and muted blues of foliage, the danger of spinifex, draping sparseness of needle pine. One lone sand wattle is a true survivor. Its roots form a frame out from the sand dune like a gnarled hand reaching deep into a well for water. Over time the wind changes everything. Sand sculptures keeping shifting. New fragments of ancient bone will be discovered.

just a spec standing
on an ancient landscape
dreaming

artist's dream –
spring spinifex in sun

between cloud fragments
you'll find me floating

wallpaper sky –
every cloud repeats itself

jasmine on the dashboard
inner city spring

spring graffiti –
blossom all over
the warehouse wall

solitary –
one rose pink cloud

spring nest–
blackbirds upcycle
a soft clump of hair

stamped
on a city wall
a white space sky

frog-filled verges –
we wait
for meteor showers
under a night sky
scraped with clouds

swinging legs
over the pier
we sat in silence
and watched waterbirds
change shape

Brunswick evening
air heavy with spring –
they spoke
to each other
in clarinet

playing poetry on clarinet
a handful
of my favourite
F sharp minor notes –
the way the rain falls

floating away

with the night
clouds

and tiny
city stars

blossom
in the wind
how far
I have travelled
in one place

Barkly Street Footscray –
air so quiet but loud
with evening spices

introvert's paradise –
no one else in the cinema

dusk –
walking about
with the magpies

rose petals
lying in shade
or catching the sun
we go the way
of flowers

ankle-deep
in orange nasturtiums
spinning a paper daisy sun
a poet's voice
in a room crowded with flowers

grateful
for this moment
in time –
a bee crawls inside
a correa bell

frogs and stars
everywhere –
the night
settles in
by the river

SWAN LAKE
AN INTROVERT'S
KIND OF CROWD
R.C

embodied
inside raindrops
tiny dreams

quiet spaces –
the turmoil
of missing someone

sunday news –
the shifting shape
of one small cloud

droplets of rain
settle the sway
of wild grasses

climate change –
removing my glasses
so I don't see the future

arrival of shorebirds –
a happy global constant

classrooms must have
daydream windows
and five
rainbow lorikeets
in the apple tree

device free
we trace a branch
to a burl and roll
into the shifting
shade

bare feet
on the new slab –
dreaming of windows
which will frame
the moon

forgotten passwords
but I always
know who I am

rain on the roof
                    just rain

melancholy   sky

by the window
drinking
moonbeams –
the only thing
on my mind

on the fence
a marbled gecko
painted in moonlight –
I pace warm air
bare feet on bricks

sliding door
wide open
the soft a cappella
of doves
fills the room

after the party
by the open window
of dusk
the scent
of a new book

quiet morning
the streets all
hung over

outside
our new window
the little blackbird
who always
visits

curled
in paving sand
little dog
basking
in morning sun

inside Nana's
blue glass swan
a small child
drifts away
somewhere

ethereal –
an egret flies
into the fog

empty shells –
the ocean
in my coat pocket

moon in a roadside puddle
already back
in the sky

letting thoughts fly the hollow bones of birds

crickets sing softly
and the moon
ripples across
the old shed roof –
brushstrokes for dreaming

look
the whole world
inside a raindrop
clinging
to a leaf

freight train
those tiny stars
so far away

scattered stars –
wind sweeps
the canopy

rainforest secrets
the silent drift
of spores

nearly midnight
the rain dances
all around me

heavy rain
on our tin roof
stars travel
out to sea

cycling along
the river bank
our spokes collecting
morning sun –
the Earth spins

open window
a little stardust
with the breeze

hot autumn night
cricket song
from the old floorboards

distant train
the night travels on

mossoftensenses

regenerating my life with trees

Acknowledgements

Poems in this book have appeared in the following publications:

'jasmine on the dash' and 'industrial skyline': *Wild Plum*, a haiku journal

'Hearts': *Pink Cover Zine*, Issue 3

'between the lines', 'stamped on a city sky' and 'arrival of shorebirds': *Failed haiku,* A journal of English senryu

'along the track' and 'rain soaked moss': *Windfall,* Australian haiku

'Brunswick evening': *Eucalypt*, a tanka journal

'inside Nana's': *Not Very Quiet*, a twice-yearly journal for women's poetry

'letting thoughts fly': *Human/Kind Journal of Topical and Contemporary Japanese Short-forms and Art*

Photos and Artwork

Front cover and page 7: Tottenham railyards, West Footscray, Melbourne
Page 19: haiga – Tarra-Bulga National Park, South Gippsland, Victoria
Page 20: Tarra-Bulga National Park
Page 22: Tarra-Bulga National Park
Page 31: West Footscray, Melbourne
Page 33: linocut haiga
Page 40: linocut collage haiga
Page 56: Tarra-Bulga National Park

www.ingramcontent.com/pod-product-compliance
Lightning Source LLC
Chambersburg PA
CBHW062203100526
44589CB00014B/1926
* 9 7 8 1 7 6 0 4 1 9 2 1 9 *